TOFU AT CENTER STAGE

Recipes by Gary Landgrebe
Illustrations by Seraphina Landgrebe

fresh
press

May all we do
        Be sung as songs of praise
                to Yahweh, His Christ, and Holy Spirit.

A special thanks to Seraphina, Junauro and Oradona for their constantly loving support; to Sharon for being willing to share her experience; to all of you who have given such overwhelming encouragement by your willingness to change; and most of all, to You Father, without Whom there would be truly nothing.

Copyright © Gary Landgrebe, 1981

Published by Fresh Press
            774 Allen Court
            Palo Alto, California 94303

To order by mail send your name and address along with a check for $6.70 ($7.00 if you live in California) to Fresh Press at the above address.

Library of Congress Number: 80-69560
ISBN: 0-9601398-3-4

First Edition: February 1981

TOFU AT CENTER STAGE

CONTENTS

ABOUT TOFU AT CENTER STAGE

TOFU AT CENTER STAGE has been designed to make trying new recipes easy and fun. Its type style (Souvenir) and its recipe layout work together to make the doing easy. Since all Fresh Press recipes are tested nearly half a dozen times before being chosen for publication, cooking is fun because you know your efforts in the kitchen will be successful and satisfying.

In each section of TOFU AT CENTER STAGE, the recipes are ordered according to preparation time. If you are pushed for time, look toward the beginning of a section for a quick, tasty entree. On more leisurely days, explore the suggestions farther on in the chapters. You may also notice that the recipes tend to be grouped according to stove-top or oven use. To help conserve energy, choose an oven entree to accompany a baked veggie or dessert.

Because we know that some people, for one reason or another, feel uncomfortable with meatless meals, and because we are eager for everyone to experience tofu, we have included a few recipes combining tofu with fish and with ecologically/nutritionally sound range-fed beef or beefalo. Both range-fed beef and beefalo fit naturally into our earth's food chain. They roam rangelands of little agricultural value, eating grasses which humans cannot digest. In so doing, they convert humanly useless substances into protein that may be used to nourish our bodies.* Range-fed beef and/or beefalo are readily available in most natural food stores and health food stores. Neither is widely advertised yet by supermarkets. However, many supermarkets do carry New Zealand beef—which is range-fed. Ask your local butcher about the source of the beef he sells.

In the two years since TOFU GOES WEST was published, more and more people all over the United States have been discovering

*See DIET FOR A SMALL PLANET, "The Hidden Talent of Livestock", by Frances Moore Lappé, for more information.

tofu and looking for tasty ways to incorporate it into their everyday diets. TOFU AT CENTER STAGE is our response to this increasing interest in, and need for, good recipes using this excellent food. We hope you enjoy the recipes selected for TOFU AT CENTER STAGE as much as people have been enjoying those in TOFU GOES WEST.

Sharon Elliot
Fresh Press

USING TOFU

TOFU

The process by which tofu is made is centuries old. Today's modern machinery has simplified the work but the ingredients and techniques remain unchanged. First, soybeans are soaked in water and blended to a fine pureé. Then the mixture is boiled and strained through very fine cheesecloth. The strained liquid, called soy milk, is brought to a simmer for a short time. A natural coagulant (usually calcium sulfate, calcium lactate or nigari) is then added. This causes the soy milk to separate into curds and whey— just as dairy milk separates when rennet is added in the production of cheese. The filtered curds are pressed into molds and chilled to give the tofu (soy cheese) its familiar shape.

PURCHASING TOFU

The tofu called for in TOFU AT CENTER STAGE is fresh, white and custard-like. It comes in many forms—from very soft to quite firm. It may be packaged in water in rectangular shaped tubs or vacuum packed as natural cheeses often are. All these types of tofu may be used successfully in TOFU AT CENTER STAGE recipes. They do differ considerably in flavor and texture, however, so experiment with them to see if you have a preference.

The weight of packaged tofu varies considerably from brand to brand. Common weights include 8 oz., 12 oz., 16 oz. (1 lb.), and 22 oz. You may find it necessary to use more or less than one package in a TOFU AT CENTER STAGE recipe. For example, if you have a 22 oz. package and are making a recipe that calls for one pound of tofu, use ¾ of the block. (See "STORING TOFU" for information on how to keep the remaining tofu.)

Take time to become familiar with the date coding used for the tofu made in your area. Freshness influences the taste of tofu greatly. When fresh, tofu is very mild. As it ages, it takes on a distinctive tang. Use only the freshest tofu for desserts and subtly spiced main dishes.

STORING TOFU

Tofu may be refrigerated in its original, unopened container for 7–10 days. Once opened, it should be rinsed well, immersed in water, covered and refrigerated until needed. The water should be changed daily.

FROZEN TOFU

Tofu may be frozen in its original container or in other convenient sized packages. When tofu has been frozen for a week or more, its texture is transformed from creamy-smooth to spongelike. It can then be crumbled or sliced and used as a substitute for meat or pasta.

When frozen tofu is used, it should be thawed thoroughly, rinsed well, and squeezed dry. Frozen tofu can be thawed at room temperature in 8–12 hours. To thaw it more quickly, remove it from its package by running warm tap water over it. Place it in a pan and cover it with water. Bring it to a boil and simmer, covered, until no ice crystals are felt when a knife is inserted in the center (about 30 minutes).

Recipes calling for frozen tofu in TOFU AT CENTER STAGE always list it in terms of its weight before freezing.

WEIGHTWATCHER'S DELIGHT

Tofu is a perfect diet food. Low calorie cooking classes across the country are discovering that an eight-ounce serving of tofu costs the weightwatcher only 147–168 calories while supplying over one quarter of an adult male's recommended protein portion for a day. Tofu also provides an abundance of calcium and iron as well as a plethora of other minerals and vitamins.

DIGESTION MADE EASY

All the difficult to digest crude fibers found in soybeans are automatically removed during the production of tofu. This makes tofu an ideal food for those with special digestive needs, including babies and surgical recuperees.

A WORD FROM THE AUTHOR

Until recently many of us have considered our Western diets ideal. Faced with mounting evidence to the contrary, however, it is becoming difficult to maintain our enthusiasm. Continued reports of starvation in many parts of our world, warnings about health problems resulting from heavy reliance on meat for nourishment, and rising costs of traditional protein staples are causing us to seek alternatives. We are facing another kind of energy crisis; one that concerns our very bodies. We must reexamine our needs, weigh our resources, and make the best use of what's available.

America is presently the world's largest producer of soybeans. However, most of these are not used as primary foods for humans, but are needlessly and inefficiently wasted fattening livestock during their last few weeks of life. (Eight to eighteen pounds of soybeans are required to produce one pound of fat in beef.) Eliminating this last minute fattening process would benefit us in two ways. First, it would release the soybean harvest for human consumption and second, it would make wholesome, less costly, range-fed meat available to the purchaser.

The hour has come for the soybean to avail the world of its splendid possibilities. In the U.S., the soy food, tofu, offers us a high protein, low calorie diet nutritionally superior to our present standard at a fraction of the cost. In other parts of our world, direct use of the soybean could actually supply the calories and other nutrients necessary to eliminate the starvation-malnutrition syndrome that plagues the earth today.

I forsee a time when we will live in harmony on the earth. The coming age will be blessed with a population that lives from the heart and considers the fate of each brother and sister as important as his own. It will be a time when every man, choosing to live by the will of God dwelling in his heart, fearlessly acts for the benefit of all.

The New Earth can be actualized only when each person sees himself as a piece of a Whole much greater than himself, as a cell in the very Body of God. Understanding that suffering parts affect the entire Being, we will realize that solely by healing others is it possible to nurture ourselves.

As a step toward this age blessed with abundance, we commend tofu to you. Tofu grants us the opportunity to share the wealth that the earth is now capable of providing.

We are a world in transition, one in which many responsible choices must be made for the benefit of all. With TOFU GOES WEST and TOFU AT CENTER STAGE we aspire to help make our food choices and changes a joy to make.

By expanding our dietary horizons, resources will be released for the benefit of mankind. Isaiah promises: "If you cease to pervert justice. . . . if you feed the hungry from your own plenty and satisfy the needs of the wretched, then your light will rise like the dawn and your dusk will be like noonday; the Lord will be your guide continually . . ." (Isaiah 56:6–11). Making use of the new world's foods is a step in a grand adventure: the rebuilding of the earth as a center in the universe where a Love Divine can truly manifest itself in the hearts, minds, and actions of each of us.

Gary Landgrebe

TOFU MAIN DISHES

INSTANT LOW CALORIE DIP

Mix in a blender until smooth
    8 OZ. VERY FRESH TOFU
    1 CUP YOGURT (OR ½ CUP *EACH* YOGURT AND
    SOUR CREAM)
    1 PACKET (4 SERVING SIZE) ONION SOUP MIX

Makes 2 cups.

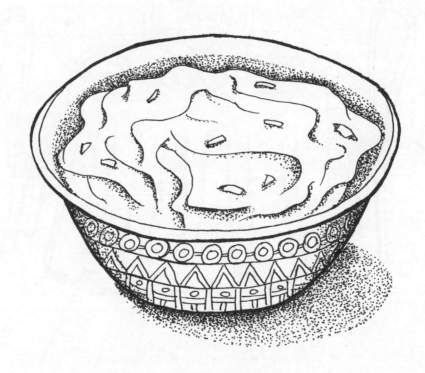

MOCKAMOLÉ

Blend in a blender until smooth
    ½ CAN (7 OZ.) CHILI SALSA (RESERVE REMAINING
      SALSA)
    ½ LB. VERY FRESH TOFU
    2 TBS. LEMON JUICE
    ½ TSP. SALT
    1 TSP. *EACH* GARLIC POWDER AND CHILI POWDER
    2 TSP. ONION POWDER

Stir in with a long handled spoon
    REMAINING CHILI SALSA
    1 CUP YOGURT

Refrigerate for several hours before serving.
Serve with natural corn chips or crisp veggies.

QUICK CURRIED TOFU SPREAD OR SANDWICH FILLING

Mix well in a medium-sized bowl

    1 LB. VERY FRESH TOFU, MASHED WELL WITH A FORK OR A POTATO MASHER

    2-4 TBS. MAYONNAISE

    2 TSP. MEAT OR VEGETABLE FLAVORED BOUILLON

    ¼ TSP. CURRY POWDER

Refrigerate for several hours before serving.

SUSHI GOES WEST

THE FILLING

Mix well in a medium-sized bowl
>   8 OZ. VERY FRESH TOFU, MASHED WELL WITH A
>   FORK OR A POTATO MASHER
>   ½ CUP GRATED CHEDDAR CHEESE
>   1 CUP COOKED RICE, CHILLED
>   ¼–½ CUP CHOPPED GREEN ONIONS
>   2 TBS. GRATED GINGER ROOT
>   2 TBS. SOY SAUCE

THE SUSHI

4 SHEETS OF NORI (AVAILABLE FROM JAPANESE
   SPECIALITY GROCERS)

Spoon one-fourth of the filling in a line near the edge of each sheet.
Roll the sheet around the filling.
Cut each roll in half with a very sharp knife.

Serves 2 as a main dish, 4–8 as a side dish.

TOFU JOE'S

Sauté in a large skillet for about 3 minutes
   1 CUP CHOPPED ONION
   1 CUP CHOPPED GREEN PEPPER

In
   2 TBS. BUTTER

Add and sauté for 2 minutes more
   2 CUPS SLICED MUSHROOMS

Stir in
   1 CAN (15 OZ.) TOMATO SAUCE
   ⅓ CUP CATSUP
   2 LBS. TOFU, MASHED WELL WITH A FORK OR A
      POTATO MASHER
   1 TBS. + 2 TSP. BEEF FLAVORED BOUILLON
   1 TSP. CHILI POWDER
   ¾ TSP. LIQUID HOT PEPPER SEASONING (OPTIONAL)

Simmer for 5 minutes.

Ladle over buttered toast or bread.
Serves 4.

TOFU TACO OPEN-FACED SANDWICHES

Sauté until limp
>   1 LARGE ONION, CHOPPED

In
>   1-2 TBS. OLIVE OIL

Stir in
>   1 CAN (8 OZ.) TOMATO SAUCE
>   1 CAN (7 OZ.) GREEN CHILI SALSA
>   2 LBS. TOFU, MASHED WELL WITH A FORK OR A
>   POTATO MASHER
>   2 TBS. SLICED GREEN OLIVES
>   1 TBS. + 2 TSP. BEEF FLAVORED BOUILLON
>   1½ TSP. CHILI POWDER
>   ½ TSP. *EACH* CUMIN AND GARLIC POWDER

Bring to a boil, reduce heat, and simmer 5-10 minutes.
Ladle over lightly toasted hamburger buns or bread.

Garnish with
>   SHREDDED CHEESE
>   SHREDDED ICEBERG LETTUCE
>   CHOPPED TOMATOES
>   AVOCADO SLICES
>   SOUR CREAM

Serves 4-6.

QUICK TOFU CURRY

Brown lightly in a large skillet with a cover
　　　1 LARGE ONION, THINLY SLICED
　　　2-3 CLOVES GARLIC, MINCED

In
　　　2 TBS. OIL

Reduce heat to low.

Add and continue cooking, stirring constantly, for 2 minutes
　　　¼ CUP CATSUP
　　　THE SPICE MIXTURE (RECIPE FOLLOWS)

Stir in
　　　1 CUP WATER
　　　2 LBS. TOFU, MASHED WELL WITH A FORK OR A
　　　　POTATO MASHER
　　　¼ CUP RAISINS (*OR* 2 TBS. *EACH* RAISINS AND
　　　　CHOPPED DRIED APPLES)
　　　3 TBS. HONEY
　　　1 TBS. + 1 TSP. CHICKEN FLAVORED BOUILLON

Bring to a boil, reduce heat and simmer, covered, for 10 minutes.
Stir once.
Ladle over rice or millet. Pass the chutney and curds (yogurt).
Serves 4.

SPICE MIXTURE

Mix well in a small bowl
    2 TBS. CURRY
    1½ TSP. GINGER
    1 TSP. SALT
    ¾ TSP. GARLIC POWDER
    ¾ TSP. CINNAMON
    ½ TSP. CUMIN
    ¼ TSP. CLOVES

RICE AND TOFU ESPAÑOL

Sauté in a large, heavy skillet with a cover
> 1 LARGE ONION, COARSELY CHOPPED
> 1 CUP CHOPPED GREEN PEPPER
> 2 CLOVES GARLIC, MINCED OR PRESSED

In
> 2–3 TBS. OIL

Add and bring to a boil
> 1 CAN (16 OZ.) STEWED TOMATOES
> 2 CUPS WATER
> 1½ LBS. TOFU, MASHED WELL WITH A FORK OR A
>   POTATO MASHER
> 1 TBS. + 1 TSP. BEEF FLAVORED BOUILLON
> 2 TSP. CHILI POWDER
> 1 TSP. CUMIN
> 1 TSP. OREGANO
> ½ TSP. SALT

Stir in
> 1 CUP CONVERTED RICE

Return to a boil, reduce heat and simmer, covered, for 20 minutes.
Remove from heat.
Let stand for 5 minutes before uncovering.
Serves 4.

STUFFED MUSHROOMS

Mix well in a large bowl
>   1 LB. TOFU, MASHED WELL WITH A FORK OR A
>   POTATO MASHER
>   1 EGG, LIGHTLY BEATEN
>   ¼ CUP GRATED PARMESAN CHEESE
>   3 TBS. MELTED BUTTER
>   2 TBS. FINELY CHOPPED PARSLEY
>   1 TSP. GARLIC POWDER
>   ¾ TSP. SALT
>   ½ TSP. BASIL
>   ¼ TSP. *EACH* PAPRIKA AND PEPPER

Clean and stem
>   1 LB. LARGE MUSHROOMS

Stuff the stem cavities with mounds of the tofu mixture.
Dust with
>   PAPRIKA

Bake at 350° for 20 minutes in a buttered baking dish.
Delicious warm or chilled.

ORIENTAL SKILLET

Steam just enough to defrost and separate
　　10 OZ. FROZEN CHOPPED SPINACH

Sauté for 3 minutes in a large oven-proof skillet
　　1 LARGE ONION, THINLY SLICED
　　1 SMALL GREEN PEPPER, CHOPPED

In
　　2 TBS. OIL

Add and sauté for 2 minutes more
　　1 CUP SLICED MUSHROOMS, PACKED
　　¼ CUP CHOPPED WALNUTS

Remove from heat.

Stir in
　　1 LB. TOFU, MASHED WELL WITH A FORK OR A
　　　　POTATO MASHER
　　2 CUPS COOKED RICE OR MILLET
　　THE STEAMED SPINACH
　　2 TBS. *EACH* SOY SAUCE AND HONEY
　　1 TBS. CHICKEN FLAVORED BOUILLON
　　4 EGGS, LIGHTLY BEATEN

Bake at 350° for 30–35 minutes.
Serves 4.

TOFU NOODLE SKILLET

Sauté in a large oven-proof skillet with a cover
    1 LARGE ONION, CHOPPED
    1 MEDIUM BELL PEPPER, CHOPPED
    1 CUP CHOPPED CELERY

In
    1–2 TBS. BUTTER

Add
    1 CAN (16 OZ.) TOMATOES, BROKEN UP
    1 CAN (8 OZ.) TOMATO SAUCE
    1 TBS. + 1 TSP. BEEF FLAVORED BOUILLON
    1½ CUPS WATER
    ¾ TSP. GARLIC POWDER
    1 TBS. HONEY
    1 TSP. SALT
    ¼ TSP. PEPPER
    8 OZ. FINE EGG NOODLES (UNCOOKED)
Bring to a simmer, stirring regularly.

Add
    1 LB. TOFU, MASHED WELL WITH A FORK OR A
      POTATO MASHER
Bring again to a simmer, stirring constantly.

Top with
    4 HARD BOILED EGGS, CRUMBLED
Dust with
    PAPRIKA

Bake, covered, at 350° for 35 minutes.
Serves 4 generously.

ZUCCHINI HERB CASSEROLE

Sauté in a large oven-proof skillet with a cover
    1½ LBS. ZUCCHINI, CUT IN ¼" CUBES
    1½ CUPS CHOPPED GREEN ONIONS
    4 CLOVES GARLIC, PRESSED

In
    2 TBS. OIL

Cover and simmer gently for 7–10 minutes—until the zucchini is barely tender.
Remove from heat.

Stir in
    2 TSP. GARLIC SALT
    1 TSP. *EACH* BASIL AND OREGANO
    ½ TSP. PAPRIKA
    ¼ TSP. PEPPER
    2 CUPS CHOPPED TOMATOES
    1 CUP COOKED RICE OR MILLET
    1 LB. TOFU, MASHED WELL WITH A FORK OR A
        POTATO MASHER
    1 EGG, LIGHTLY BEATEN
    2 CUPS GRATED SHARP CHEDDAR CHEESE

Top with
    1 CUP GRATED SHARP CHEDDAR CHEESE
Bake at 350° for 35 minutes.
Let stand for 10 minutes before serving.
Serves 4–6.

SPROUTED VEGETABLE SKILLET

Sauté for about 5 minutes in a large oven-proof skillet over medium heat

>½ LB. MUSHROOMS, THINLY SLICED
>½ LB. BEAN SPROUTS
>½ CUP CHOPPED GREEN ONIONS

In

>3 TBS. BUTTER

Remove from heat.
Stir in

>3 TBS. CHOPPED PARSLEY
>2 TSP. BASIL
>½ TSP. SALT
>¼ TSP. PEPPER
>¾ CUP SOUR CREAM OR YOGURT
>2 EGGS, LIGHTLY BEATEN
>1 LB. TOFU, MASHED WELL WITH A FORK OR A POTATO MASHER
>3 CUPS GRATED SHARP CHEDDAR CHEESE
>⅓ CUP VEGEBACON (OPTIONAL)

Bake at 375° for 40–45 minutes.
Let stand for 10 minutes before serving.
Serves 4–6.

ARGENTINE CORN PIE

Sauté in a large oven-proof skillet over medium heat
>   1 LARGE ONION, FINELY CHOPPED
>   ½ CUP FINELY CHOPPED BELL PEPPER

In
>   1-3 TBS. OIL

Remove from heat.

Stir in
>   1 CAN (17 OZ.) WHOLE KERNEL CORN, UNDRAINED
>   1 CAN (8 OZ.) TOMATO SAUCE
>   1 LB. TOFU, MASHED WELL WITH A FORK OR A
>   POTATO MASHER
>   ½ CUP RAISINS
>   2 TSP. BEEF FLAVORED BOUILLON
>   1½ TSP. CUMIN
>   1 TSP. *EACH* GARLIC POWDER AND PAPRIKA
>   ¼-½ TSP. CAYENNE
>   ½ CUP INSTANT NONFAT MILK POWDER
>   3 EGGS, LIGHTLY BEATEN
>   1 TBS. FLOUR

Top with
    ½ CUP SLICED BLACK OLIVES
    ½ CUP CHOPPED GREEN ONIONS (INCLUDING TOPS)

Bake at 350° for 40 minutes.
Let stand for 15 minutes before serving.

Garnish with

    2 HARD BOILED EGGS, SLICED IN ROUNDS

Serves 6.

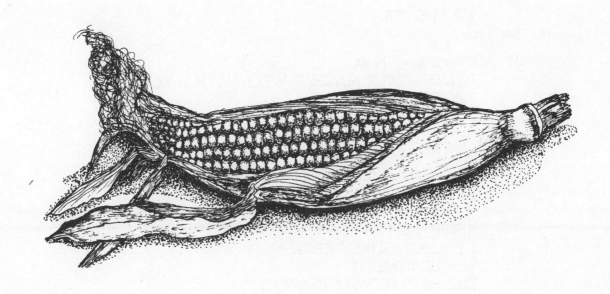

TOFU TIMBALLO WITH CHEESE SAUCE

Prepare following label instructions
>   8 OZ. SPAGHETTI, BROKEN TO ½ STRANDS

Drain well.

Toss with
>   ¼ CUP MELTED BUTTER

Set aside.

Sauté until limp
>   ⅓ CUP FINELY CHOPPED ONION
>   1½–2 CUPS SLICED MUSHROOMS

In
>   1–2 TBS. OIL

Set aside.

Mix well in a large bowl
>   1½ LBS. TOFU, MASHED WELL WITH A FORK OR A
>   POTATO MASHER
>   1 TBS. + 1 TSP. CHICKEN FLAVORED BOUILLON

Add
>   ½ CUP GRATED PARMESAN CHEESE
>   ⅓ CUP CHOPPED PIMIENTO STUFFED GREEN OLIVES
>   3 TBS. CHOPPED PARSLEY
>   ½ TSP. SALT
>   ¼ TSP. PEPPER
>   2 EGGS, LIGHTLY BEATEN
>   THE SPAGHETTI
>   THE SAUTÉED VEGETABLES

Toss well.

Dust a buttered 9″ spring form pan with
     ¼ CUP VERY FINE DRIED BREAD CRUMBS
Turn half the tofu mixture into the pan.

Cover with
     4 OZ. SHREDDED MOZZARELLA CHEESE

Spread the remaining tofu mixture over the shredded cheese.
Sprinkle with
     ¼ CUP VERY FINE DRIED BREAD CRUMBS

Bake at 375° for 40 minutes.
Let stand for 10 minutes before removing from the pan.

Good served with CHEESE SAUCE. (RECIPE FOLLOWS)
Serves 6–8.

CHEESE SAUCE

Mix until smooth in a small saucepan
     ¼ CUP MILK
     1 TBS. ARROWROOT OR CORNSTARCH

Add
     ¾ CUP MILK
     2 TBS. BUTTER
     ¼ CUP GRATED PARMESAN CHEESE
     1 TBS. CHOPPED PARSLEY
     ¼ TSP. SALT
     ⅛ TSP. PEPPER

Bring to a boil and simmer, stirring constantly, until thickened
(about 2 minutes).

TOFU LOAF

Mix well in a large bowl
    1½ LBS. TOFU, MASHED WITH A FORK OR A POTATO MASHER
    3 EGGS, LIGHTLY BEATEN
    4 SLICES FRESH BREAD, CRUMBED
    1 PACKET (FOUR SERVING SIZE) ONION SOUP MIX
    1 TBS. DEHYDRATED ONION FLAKES
    1 TSP. BEEF FLAVORED BOUILLON
    ¼ TSP. *EACH* GARLIC POWDER AND PEPPER
    1 CAN (4 OZ.) MUSHROOMS, DRAINED AND SLICED (OPTIONAL)

Turn into a buttered 9"x5" loaf pan.
Bake at 350° for 55 minutes.

Serve with GRAVY IN A SNAP* or your favorite gravy.
Makes 4 servings.

*See following page.

GRAVY IN A SNAP

Mix well in a small saucepan
      2 TBS. CORNSTARCH OR ARROWROOT
      ¼ CUP MILK

Add

      1¾ CUPS MILK
      2 TBS. SOY SAUCE
      ½ TSP. WORCHESTERSHIRE SAUCE
      ¼ TSP. PEPPER
      ⅛ TSP. GARLIC POWDER

Bring to a boil and simmer, stirring constantly, until thickened (about 2 minutes).
Remove from heat.

Add

      2 TBS. BUTTER
Stir until the butter is melted and well integrated with the other ingredients.
Makes about 2 cups gravy.

PEPPER POT

Sauté in a large oven-proof skillet with a cover
  2 LARGE ONIONS, THINLY SLICED
  3 CUPS CHOPPED MILDLY HOT PEPPERS (ANAHEIM,
     CUBANELLE, YELLOW WAX), SEEDED
  8 CLOVES GARLIC, MINCED OR PRESSED

In
  2 TBS. OLIVE OIL

Stir in
  1 CAN (15 OZ.) TOMATO SAUCE
  1 CUP WATER
  2 TSP. BEEF FLAVORED BOUILLON
  ½ TSP. SALT
Bring to a boil, reduce heat, and simmer, covered, for 5 minutes.
Remove from heat.

Stir in
  1 LB. TOFU, MASHED WELL WITH A FORK OR A
     POTATO MASHER
  1 CUP GRATED SHARP CHEDDAR CHEESE
  4 EGGS, LIGHTLY BEATEN

Bake at 375° for 1 hour.
Good served with sour cream.
Serves 6.

BAKED TOFU STEAKS

Drain
>2 LBS. FIRM TOFU

Cut each section in half vertically *and* horizontally to make four pieces approximately ½"x1¼"x2½".
Set aside.

Mix in a small bowl
>1 CUP SOY SAUCE
>3 CLOVES GARLIC, MINCED
>1 TBS. FLAVORFUL OIL (PEANUT, SESAME, TOASTED
>   SESAME)
>2 TBS. *EACH* VINEGAR AND HONEY

Pour the soy sauce mixture into an 12"x15" baking dish.
Marinate the tofu for 1–4 hours, turning occasionally.
Place the marinated tofu on a lightly oiled baking sheet.
Bake at 500° for 35–60 minutes, turning once halfway through the baking time.

Serves 4.
Good hot or cold—great for picnics!

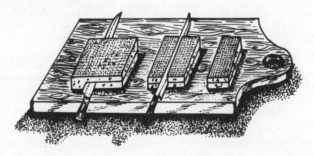

CHEESE ONION PIE

THE CRUST (OPTIONAL)

Prepare your favorite unsweetened, single, 10″ crust.
Prick well with a fork.
Bake at 425° for 7 minutes.

THE FILLING

Sauté

> 1 MEDIUM ONION, CHOPPED

In

> 1–2 TBS. OIL

Spread the onion evenly on the bottom of the crust or in the bottom of a buttered 10″ baking dish.

Mix in a blender until smooth
> 1 CUP BUTTERMILK
> 2 EGG YOLKS
> 1½ LBS. TOFU
> 1 TSP. VEGETABLE FLAVORED BOUILLON
> 1 TBS. DEHYDRATED ONION FLAKES
> 2 TBS. FLOUR
> ¾ TSP. SALT
> ½ TSP. PAPRIKA
> ¼ TSP. PEPPER

Add and mix in well with a long handled spoon
    2 CUPS GRATED CHEDDAR CHEESE

Spread gently over the onions.
Bake at 350° for 45 minutes.

Beat until light and frothy in a medium bowl
    2 EGG WHITES

Add and beat in
    ¼ CUP GRATED PARMESAN CHEESE

Remove pie from oven and spread with the beaten egg white mixture.
Return to the oven for an additional 15 minutes.
Serves 6–8.

FROZEN TOFU MAIN DISHES

EGG SALAD

Mix well in a large bowl
     6 TBS. MAYONNAISE (OR MORE, TO TASTE)
     ½ TSP. SALT
     ⅛ TSP. PEPPER
     1 TBS. CHOPPED ONION
     2 TBS. DICED RADISH
     ½ CUP *EACH* DICED CELERY AND CUCUMBER
     1 LB. FROZEN TOFU, THAWED, RINSED, SQUEEZED
DRY AND CRUMBLED
     3 HARD BOILED EGGS, CHOPPED

Serve on crisp lettuce leaves.
Makes 3–4 servings.

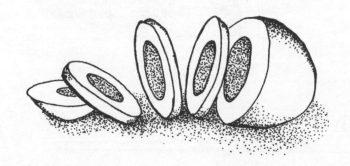

OPEN-FACED TOFU SALAD SANDWICHES

Mix well in a large bowl
- ¼ CUP MAYONNAISE
- 2 TBS. LEMON JUICE
- ½ TSP. SALT
- ¼ TSP. LIQUID HOT PEPPER SEASONING
- ¼ TSP. PEPPER
- 1 CAN (9½ OZ.) WATER CHESTNUTS, DRAINED AND CHOPPED
- ½ CUP CHOPPED GREEN ONIONS
- 1 LB. FROZEN TOFU, THAWED, RINSED, SQUEEZED DRY AND CRUMBLED

Serve bedded on crisp shredded lettuce atop toasted, buttered English muffins.

Makes 8 sandwiches, serves 4.

MINTED TOFU SALAD

Mix well in a large bowl
> 1 LB. FROZEN TOFU, THAWED, RINSED, SQUEEZED
>   DRY AND CRUMBLED
> 1½ CUPS COOKED MILLET
> 1 CUP FROZEN PEAS, THAWED
> 1 CUP THINLY SLICED CELERY
> 3 TBS. CHOPPED GREEN ONIONS
> 2 TBS. CHOPPED PARSLEY
> 2 TBS. CHOPPED FRESH MINT
> 3 TBS. LIME JUICE
> ¾ TSP. SALT
> ½ TSP. GRATED LIME PEEL (OR LEMON PEEL)
> ¼ TSP. PEPPER

Stir in
> SPECIAL DRESSING (RECIPE FOLLOWS)

Turn into a salad bowl lined with
> CRISP LETTUCE LEAVES

Garnish with
> MINT SPRIGS

Serves 2–3.

SPECIAL DRESSING

Mix well in a medium-sized bowl
    ½ CUP MAYONNAISE
    ¼ CUP BUTTERMILK
    1 TBS. HONEY
    1 TSP. DIJON MUSTARD
    ½ TSP. LIQUID HOT PEPPER SEASONING

TOFU ALA CARBONARA

Beat in a small mixing bowl for 1 minute
        2 EGGS
Set aside.

Bring to a boil in a medium-sized saucepan
        2 LBS. FROZEN TOFU, THAWED, RINSED, SQUEEZED
          DRY, AND CRUMBLED
        1 CLOVE GARLIC, MINCED OR PRESSED
        WATER TO COVER
Turn into a strainer and press dry with a spoon.

Mix well in a large bowl
        THE HOT FROZEN TOFU
        THE BEATEN EGGS
        ¼ CUP MELTED BUTTER
        ¾–1 CUP VEGEBACON
        ½ CUP GRATED PARMESAN CHEESE
        ⅓ CUP FINELY CHOPPED PARSLEY

Serve immediately.
Makes 6 servings.

HOT POTATO SALAD

Steam until tender
>   5 CUPS DICED POTATOES (2–3 POTATOES)

Mix well in a large bowl
>   1 CUP *EACH* CHOPPED CELERY AND CHOPPED
>   GREEN ONION
>   ½ CUP CHOPPED DILL PICKLE
>   1 LB. FROZEN TOFU, THAWED, RINSED, SQUEEZED
>   DRY AND CRUMBLED
>   THE COOKED POTATOES
>   ½ CUP VEGEBACON (OPTIONAL)
>   SPECIAL BOILED DRESSING (RECIPE FOLLOWS)

Serve hot or cold.
Makes 4–6 servings.

SPECIAL BOILED DRESSING

Bring to a boil in a small saucepan, stirring constantly
>   ¼ CUP MAYONNAISE
>   3 TBS. APPLE CIDER VINEGAR
>   2 TBS. *EACH* BROWN SUGAR AND WATER
>   1 TSP. SALT

Use immediately.

SWEET AND SOUR TOFU AND PEPPERS

Sauté in a large skillet for about 2 minutes
> 2 LARGE BELL PEPPERS (GREEN, RED OR A
> COMBINATION), CUT IN ¾" PIECES

In
> 3 TBS. OIL

Remove from heat.

Mix in a small bowl until smooth
> THE LIQUID DRAINED FROM A 20 OZ. CAN OF
> JUICE-PACKED PINEAPPLE CHUNKS
> 1 TBS. ARROWROOT OR CORNSTARCH
> ¼ CUP *EACH* SOY SAUCE, HONEY AND CATSUP
> 3 TBS. *EACH* DRY SHERRY AND VINEGAR
> ¼ TSP. PEPPER

Pour the blended ingredients into the skillet.
Heat, stirring constantly, until the mixture bubbles and thickens.
Add
> 2 LBS. FROZEN TOFU, THAWED, RINSED, SQUEEZED
> DRY AND CRUMBLED
> THE PINEAPPLE CHUNKS

Cook, stirring, for 2 minutes more.

Stir in
> 2 CUPS MUNG BEAN SPROUTS

Serve over rice.
Makes 4 servings.

BARBECUED "BEEFLESS"

Sauté in a large skillet with a cover
     1 LARGE ONION, CHOPPED FINE
     1 LARGE GREEN PEPPER, CHOPPED FINE

In
     1-3 TBS. OIL

Stir in
     1 CAN (15 OZ.) TOMATO SAUCE
     1 CUP WATER
     2 TBS. *EACH* BROWN SUGAR AND VINEGAR
     1 TBS. + 1 TSP. BEEF FLAVORED BOUILLON
     1 TSP. CHILI POWDER
     ½ TSP. GARLIC POWDER
     ½ TSP. *EACH* ALLSPICE AND OREGANO
     ¼ TSP. LIQUID SMOKE
Bring to a boil, reduce heat and simmer, covered, for 8 minutes.

Add
     2 LBS. FROZEN TOFU, THAWED, RINSED, SQUEEZED
     DRY AND CRUMBLED

Mix well.
Cook, stirring constantly, until heated through.
Serves 4.

TOFU CON FETTUCINI

Prepare following label instructions
  6 OZ. MEDIUM NOODLES

While the noodles are cooking—
Sauté in a large skillet for about 2 minutes
  1 CUP CHOPPED GREEN PEPPER

In
  2 TBS. BUTTER

Add and sauté 2–3 minutes more
  8 OZ. SLICED MUSHROOMS
Stir in
  1 CUP WATER
  2 TSP. CHICKEN FLAVORED BOUILLON
  2 LBS. FROZEN TOFU, THAWED, RINSED, SQUEEZED
   DRY AND CUT IN ½″ CUBES
Cook until all liquid is absorbed.
Remove from heat.
Add
  THE NOODLES, HOT AND WELL DRAINED
  ¼ CUP MELTED BUTTER
  ½ CUP GRATED PARMESAN CHEESE
  ½ TSP. SALT
  ¼ TSP. PEPPER

Toss thoroughly.
Serve immediately.
Makes 4 servings.

MACARONI SALAD

Mix well in a large bowl

    2 CUPS COOKED MACARONI
    ½ LB. FROZEN TOFU, THAWED, RINSED, SQUEEZED
      DRY AND CRUMBLED
    2 HARD BOILED EGGS, CHOPPED
    ¼ CUP FINELY CHOPPED GREEN ONIONS
    ¼ CUP FINELY CHOPPED CELERY
    ¼ CUP FINELY CHOPPED DILL PICKLE
    1 MEDIUM TOMATO, FINELY CHOPPED
    2 TBS. FINELY CHOPPED PARSLEY
    2-4 TBS. MAYONNAISE
    2 TSP. BEEF FLAVORED BOUILLON
    ½ TSP. PEPPER

Refrigerate for several hours before serving.
Serves 2.

ARMENIAN EGGPLANT SKILLET

Combine in a medium-sized saucepan
>1 MEDIUM EGGPLANT, DICED IN ¼″ CUBES
>¾ CUP WATER
>½ TSP. SALT

Bring to a boil, reduce heat, and simmer, covered, for 10 minutes.

While the eggplant is simmering—
Sauté for 3 minutes in a large skillet
>1 MEDIUM ONION, CHOPPED FINE
>¼ CUP CHOPPED GREEN PEPPER
>4 LARGE CLOVES GARLIC, MINCED OR PRESSED

In
>2–3 TBS. OIL

Add and sauté for 3 minutes more
>1 CUP SLICED MUSHROOMS, PACKED
>1½ TSP. CURRY
>½ TSP. PAPRIKA

Stir in
>THE EGGPLANT, UNDRAINED
>2 LBS. FROZEN TOFU, THAWED, RINSED, SQUEEZED
>   DRY AND CRUMBLED
>4–5 TSP. CHICKEN FLAVORED BOUILLON

Simmer for 3 minutes, stirring frequently.
Remove from heat and stir in
>2 EGGS, LIGHTLY BEATEN
>1 CUP SOUR CREAM

Continue stirring until the entree is smooth and thickened.
Serves 4–6. Good with millet or rice.

ONION MUSHROOM SOUP

Sauté until golden in a large skillet with a cover
>5 MEDIUM ONIONS, THINLY SLICED

In
>2–3 TBS. BUTTER

Add and sauté for 2 minutes more
>1 CUP SLICED MUSHROOMS, PACKED
>1 LB. FROZEN TOFU, THAWED, RINSED, SQUEEZED
>DRY AND CRUMBLED

Stir in
>2 QUARTS WATER
>1 TBS. + 2 TSP. BEEF FLAVORED BOUILLON

Bring to a boil, reduce heat, and simmer, covered, for 20 minutes.
Serve with
>GRATED PARMESAN CHEESE

Makes about 2 quarts.

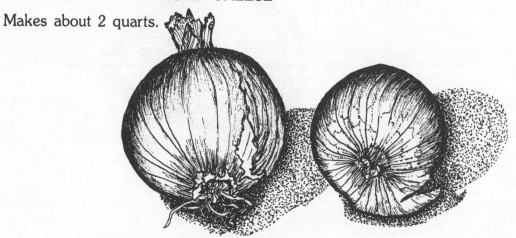

ELEGANT YAMS IN ORANGE SAUCE

Bring to a boil, reduce heat and simmer, covered, for 25 minutes
>   1½ CUPS WATER
>   1½ LBS. YAMS
>   ½ TSP. SALT

Drain the cooking liquid into a large measuring cup.
Add water to make 1½ cups liquid.

Mix in a large skillet
>   ½ CUP FROZEN ORANGE JUICE CONCENTRATE
>   ½ CUP MAJOR GREY'S CHUTNEY
>   2 TBS. BUTTER
>   1 TBS. + 1 TSP. CHICKEN FLAVORED BOUILLON
>   2 TSP. ARROWROOT OR CORNSTARCH DISSOLVED
>   IN ¼ CUP WATER
>   ½ TSP. GRATED ORANGE RIND
>   ⅛ TSP. CLOVES

Bring to a boil and simmer, stirring constantly, until thickened (about 2 minutes).

Add
>   THE YAMS, BROKEN UP
>   2 LBS. FROZEN TOFU, THAWED, RINSED, SQUEEZED
>   DRY AND CRUMBLED

Simmer for an additional 3 minutes, stirring constantly.

Garnish with
>   1-2 ORANGES, SECTIONED

Serves 4.

GADO-GADO SALAD

Steam until tender
     ⅓ LB. GREEN BEANS, CUT IN 1″ LENGTHS

Steam until limp
     10–12 OZ. SPINACH
Drain vegetables and chill thoroughly.

Toss well in a large bowl ·
     1 LB. FROZEN TOFU, THAWED, RINSED, SQUEEZED
        DRY AND CRUMBLED
     ⅓ LB. MUNG BEAN SPROUTS
     3 CUPS FINELY CHOPPED ICEBERG LETTUCE
     THE CHILLED VEGETABLES
     PEANUT DRESSING (RECIPE FOLLOWS)

Spoon onto a large decorative serving dish.
Garnish with
     THIN CUCUMBER SLICES
     2 MEDIUM TOMATOES, SLICED IN WEDGES
     4 HARD BOILED EGGS, QUARTERED

Serve immediately.
Serves 4–6.

PEANUT DRESSING

Sauté until golden
>   1 SMALL ONION, CHOPPED

In
>   2 TBS. OIL

Reduce heat to low and stir in
>   ½ CUP BOILING WATER
>   ½ CUP PEANUT BUTTER
>   ½ CUP MILK
>   2 TBS. BROWN SUGAR
>   1 TBS. LEMON JUICE
>   2 TSP. CHICKEN FLAVORED BOUILLON
>   1 TSP. SOY SAUCE
>   ½ TSP. SALT
>   ½ TSP. GINGER (OR 2 TSP. FRESHLY GRATED)
>   ¼ TSP. LIQUID HOT PEPPER SEASONING

Stir until thickened.

Remove from heat.
Stir vigorously to release heat from the dressing.
Use immediately.

STEWED TOFU MILLET MOUND

Bring to a boil in a 1 quart saucepan
> 2½ CUPS WATER
> 3 TBS. FROZEN ORANGE JUICE CONCENTRATE
> 1 TBS. BUTTER
> ½ TSP. *EACH* CINNAMON AND SALT
> ⅛ TSP. CLOVES

Stir in
> 1 CUP MILLET

Return to a boil, reduce heat and simmer, covered, for 30 minutes.

Sauté until limp in a large skillet with a cover
> 1 LARGE ONION, THINLY SLICED

In
> 1 TBS. *EACH* BUTTER AND OLIVE OIL

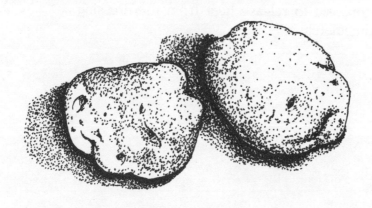

Stir in
> 4 CUPS WATER
> 3 CUPS DICED POTATOES
> 1 CUP DICED CARROT
> ¼ CUP CATSUP
> 1 TBS. + 1 TSP. BEEF FLAVORED BOUILLON
> ½ TSP. *EACH* SALT AND TUMERIC
> ¼ TSP. PEPPER
> ⅛ TSP. CAYENNE
> 2 LBS. FROZEN TOFU, THAWED, RINSED, SQUEEZED
>   DRY AND CRUMBLED

Bring to a boil, reduce heat and simmer, covered, for 20 minutes.

Stir in
> 1 CUP FROZEN PEAS

Simmer, covered, for 7 minutes more.
Remove from heat and stir in the cooked millet.
Serves 6–8.

TOFU MINESTRONE

Sauté until golden in a large skillet with a cover
  1 CUP CHOPPED ONION
  ½ CUP BROWN RICE
  2 CUPS SLICED MUSHROOMS

In
  3 TBS. OLIVE OIL

Add
  1 CAN (28 OZ.) TOMATOES, BROKEN UP
  5 CUPS WATER
  1 LARGE CARROT, THICKLY SLICED
  1 CUP THICKLY SLICED ZUCCHINI
  ¾ CUP CHOPPED CELERY
  ¾ CUP CHOPPED GREEN PEPPER
  ¼ CUP CHOPPED PARSLEY
  2 TBS. BEEF FLAVORED BOUILLON
  ½ CUP CHABLIS (OR APPLE JUICE)
  1 TSP. *EACH* BASIL, OREGANO, AND ROSEMARY
  ½ TSP. *EACH* SAVORY AND THYME
  ⅛ TSP. CAYENNE
  2 LBS. FROZEN TOFU, THAWED, RINSED, SQUEEZED
    DRY AND CRUMBLED

Bring to a boil, reduce heat and simmer, covered, for 50 minutes.
Stir occasionally.

Add
 ½ CUP CHABLIS (OPTIONAL)
Mix well.

Sprinkle with
 GRATED PARMESAN CHEESE
Serves 6.

RANCHO CASSEROLE

Sauté until lightly browned
>   1 CUP CHOPPED ONION
>   ¾ CUP CHOPPED GREEN PEPPER

In
>   1 TBS. BUTTER

Add
>   1 CAN (8 OZ.) TOMATO SAUCE
>   ⅓ CUP WATER
>   1 TBS. BEEF FLAVORED BOUILLON
>   1½ TSP. CHILI POWDER
>   ½ TSP. SALT
>   ½ TSP. *EACH* CINNAMON, CUMIN AND OREGANO

Simmer for 5 minutes, stirring frequently.

Remove from heat and stir in
>   1 LB. FROZEN TOFU, THAWED, RINSED, SQUEEZED
>   DRY AND CRUMBLED
>   1¾ CUP COOKED RICE OR MILLET
>   3 EGGS, LIGHTLY BEATEN
>   1 CAN (4½ OZ.) CHOPPED BLACK OLIVES,
>   UNDRAINED
>   2 TBS. LEMON JUICE

Turn into a buttered 2 quart-casserole with a cover.
Bake, covered, at 375° for 25 minutes.

Remove from oven and top with
>   2 MEDIUM TOMATOES, SLICED
>   1 MEDIUM AVOCADO, THINLY SLICED

Serves 4.

SHEPHERD'S PIE

Sauté for about 5 minutes over medium heat
   ½ CUP CHOPPED ONION
   ½ CUP CHOPPED CELERY

In
   1-2 TBS. BUTTER
Remove from heat.

Stir in
   2 LBS. FROZEN TOFU, THAWED, RINSED, SQUEEZED
      DRY AND CRUMBLED
   1½ CUPS GRAVY*
   1 CUP COOKED DICED CARROT
   1 TBS. + 1 TSP. BEEF FLAVORED BOUILLON
Turn into a buttered 2 quart baking dish.

Spoon evenly around the edge of the pie
   2½ CUPS MASHED POTATOES

Sprinkle the center of the pie with
   ½ CUP GRATED CHEESE

Bake at 375° for 30 minutes or until the potatoes are nicely
browned.
Makes 4 generous servings.

*See recipe page 33.

CHILI CREMA

Mix in a blender until smooth
>   1 CUP MILK
>   2 TBS. FLOUR
>   2 CANNED JALAPEÑO PEPPERS
>   1 TBS. CHICKEN FLAVORED BOUILLON
>   ½ TSP. SALT
>   ¼ TSP. PEPPER

Sauté until limp in a large oven-proof skillet
>   1 LARGE ONION, CHOPPED
>   2–3 CLOVES GARLIC, MINCED OR PRESSED

In
>   2 TBS. OIL
Remove from heat.

Stir in
>   THE BLENDED INGREDIENTS
>   2 LBS. FROZEN TOFU, THAWED, RINSED, SQUEEZED
>   DRY AND CRUMBLED
>   1½ CUPS SOUR CREAM
>   1 CAN (4½ OZ.) DICED GREEN CHILES
Bake at 350° for 30 minutes.

Remove from the oven.
Top with
>   1 CUP GRATED SHARP CHEDDAR CHEESE

Return to the oven for an additional 5–10 minutes or until the cheese has melted.
Serves 4.

CHILI-JACK SOUFFLÉ

Mix well in a small bowl
>   1 LB. FROZEN TOFU, THAWED, RINSED, SQUEEZED
>   DRY AND CRUMBLED
>   2 TBS. MELTED BUTTER
>   1 TSP. CHICKEN FLAVORED BOUILLON

Turn into a buttered 8″ square baking dish.

Layer *half* of each of the following, in order, over the tofu mixture
>   1 CAN (17 OZ.) WHOLE KERNEL CORN, DRAINED
>   1 CAN (4 OZ.) CHOPPED GREEN CHILES
>   1½ CUPS GRATED MONTEREY JACK CHEESE

Repeat the layers.

Mix in a blender until smooth
>   2 EGGS
>   8 OZ. VERY FRESH TOFU
>   ¾ CUP MILK
>   1 TSP. SALT
>   1 TSP. CHILI POWDER

Pour the fresh tofu mixture evenly over the casserole.
Pierce through the layers with a knife in several places.

Bake at 350° for 40–45 minutes.
Let stand for 10 minutes before cutting.
Serves 4–6.

MEATY MEATLESS TURNOVERS

THE CRUSTS

Prepare your favorite unsweetened pastry dough for a double crust pie.

Using a floured rolling pin, roll the dough out into a rectangle approximately 10" x 20".

Cut into eight 5" squares.

THE FILLING

Sauté for about 4 minutes

> ¼ CUP CHOPPED ONION
> 1 CLOVE GARLIC, MINCED OR PRESSED

In

> 1-3 TBS. BUTTER

Remove from heat.

Stir in

> 1 LB. FROZEN TOFU, THAWED, RINSED, SQUEEZED
>   DRY AND CRUMBLED
> ⅔ CUP GRAVY*
> 2 TSP. BEEF FLAVORED BOUILLON
> ¼ CUP FINELY CHOPPED DILL PICKLE
> ¼ TSP. PEPPER

Spoon ⅛ of the filling into the center of each pastry square.

Fold the dough over to form a triangle and press the edges together to seal.

Prick and bake on a buttered sheet at 425° for 20-25 minutes.

Good hot or cold.

Makes 8 servings.

*See recipe page 33.

THANKSGIVING PUMPKIN BAKE

THE PUMPKIN

A 4 LB. PUMPKIN

Remove top and seeds.
Replace the top and steam or bake until tender.
Spoon out pulp taking care not to break the outer shell.
Drain well reserving pulp, shell and top.

THE STUFFING

Sauté for 5 minutes
1 LARGE ONION, CHOPPED FINE
3 CLOVES GARLIC, MINCED OR PRESSED
Remove from heat.
Stir in
2 CUPS COOKED MILLET OR RICE
1 LB. FROZEN TOFU, THAWED, RINSED, SQUEEZED
DRY AND CRUMBLED
THE PUMPKIN PULP
1 CAN (8 OZ.) WATER CHESTNUTS, DRAINED AND
CHOPPED
1 CUP GRATED SHARP CHEDDAR CHEESE
3 EGGS, LIGHTLY BEATEN
1 TBS. + 2 TSP. CHICKEN FLAVORED BOUILLON
1 TSP. SAGE
½ TSP. *EACH* CORIANDER AND PEPPER

Fill the pumpkin shell with the stuffing. Replace the top.
Bake at 350° for 40 minutes.

TOFU - SEAFOOD ENTREES

FISHY FRY-UP

Sauté for 3 minutes
> 1 CUP CHOPPED GREEN ONIONS

In
> 2 TBS. OIL

Stir in
> 1 CAN (6½ OZ.) ALBACORE TUNA OR BONITA,
>   UNDRAINED
> 1 LB. FROZEN TOFU, THAWED, RINSED, SQUEEZED
>   DRY AND CRUMBLED
> 3 TBS. CHOPPED PARSLEY
> 1 TBS. A1 STEAK SAUCE
> 1 TSP. CHICKEN FLAVORED BOUILLON
> ½ TSP. SALT
> ½ TSP. CURRY
> ¼ TSP. *EACH* PAPRIKA AND PEPPER
> 1 CUP MILK

Cook, stirring constantly, until all liquids are absorbed.
Serves 4.

GRAIN CRUST PIE

THE CRUST

Mix well in a medium-sized bowl
> 1½ CUPS COOKED MILLET OR RICE
> 2 TBS. BUTTER, SOFTENED
> 1 EGG

Press into and up the sides of a 1½ quart baking dish.

THE FILLING

Mix well in a large bowl
> 8 OZ. TOFU, MASHED WELL WITH A FORK OR A
> POTATO MASHER
> 1 CUP GRATED SHARP CHEDDAR CHEESE
> 2 EGGS, LIGHTLY BEATEN
> 10 OZ. FROZEN PEAS, COOKED AND DRAINED
> 1 TBS. FINELY CHOPPED PARSLEY
> ¾ TSP. SALT
> ¼ TSP. PEPPER
> *EITHER*
> > 1 CAN (6½ OZ.) ALBACORE TUNA OR BONITA,
> > DRAINED AND CRUMBLED
> > 1 TSP. WORCHESTERSHIRE SAUCE
> *OR*
> > 1 CUP FINELY CHOPPED COOKED CHICKEN
> > 2 TSP. WORCHESTERSHIRE SAUCE

Turn into the prepared crust.
Bake at 375° for 30–35 minutes.
Serves 4.

TOFU TUNA MOLD

Soften
>   1 TBS. UNFLAVORED GELATIN

In
>   ¼ CUP WATER

Heat to dissolve completely.

Mix in a blender until smooth
>   3 TBS. LEMON JUICE
>   2-4 TBS. MAYONNAISE
>   1½ TSP. PREPARED MUSTARD
>   1 LB. VERY FRESH TOFU
>   ½ TSP. *EACH* ONION SALT AND SALT
>   ¼ TSP. PAPRIKA
>   THE GELATIN MIXTURE

Add and blend again just enough to mix in well
>   1 CAN (6½ OZ.) ALBACORE TUNA OR BONITA,
>   CRUMBLED

Stir in with a long handled spoon
>   ½ CUP FINELY CHOPPED CELERY
>   ¼ CUP FINELY CHOPPED DILL PICKLE
>   ¼ CUP FINELY CHOPPED ONION (OPTIONAL)

Pour into a mold or individual molds.

Chill thoroughly.
Unmold on crisp iceberg lettuce leaves.
Serves 4.

TOFU TUNA DIP

Prepare TOFU TUNA MOLD. Omit the gelatin mixture.
Serve with crackers and fresh vegetables.

TOFU-SHRIMP CASSEROLE

Prepare following label instructions
    3 CUPS FINE EGG NOODLES

Drain well.
Turn into a buttered 2 quart baking dish.

Sauté for about 5 minutes
    ½ CUP CHOPPED GREEN ONION
    ½ CUP CHOPPED CELERY

In
    ¼ CUP BUTTER

Mix in a small bowl until smooth
    1½ CUPS MILK
    ¼ CUP FLOUR
    2 TSP. PREPARED MUSTARD
    1½ TSP. SALT
    ¾ TSP. PARSLEY
    ¼ TSP. PEPPER

Pour the liquid ingredients into the skillet, stirring constantly.
Cook, stirring constantly, until thickened.

Remove from heat and stir in
    1 LB. TOFU, MASHED WELL WITH A FORK OR A
      POTATO MASHER
Pour the tofu mixture evenly over the noodles.

Top with
    1 CAN (4½ OZ.) SHRIMP, DRAINED

Mix well in a small bowl
    1 SLICE FRESH BREAD, CRUMBLED
    1 TBS. SOFT BUTTER
Sprinkle the crumbs over the casserole.

Bake at 400° for 20 minutes.
Serves 4.

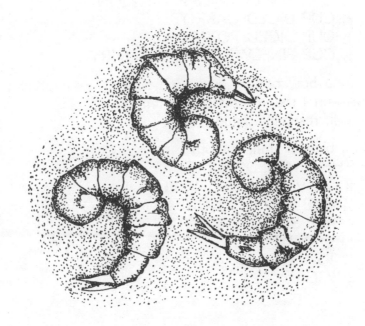

CLAM CHOWDER TORTE

THE CRUST (OPTIONAL)

Prepare your favorite unsweetened, single, 9″ crust.
Bake at 425° for 8 minutes.

THE FILLING

Drain well into a medium-sized saucepan
>   THE LIQUID FROM 2 CANS (6½ OZ.) MINCED CLAMS

Add
>   2 TBS. BUTTER
>   ¾ CUP FINELY CHOPPED ONION
>   ¾ CUP DICED CARROT
>   ¾ CUP DICED POTATO
>   ½ CUP FINELY CHOPPED CELERY

Bring to a boil, reduce heat, and simmer, covered, for 12–15
minutes—until the vegetables are tender.
Drain well, reserving liquid.

Mix in a blender until smooth
>   THE DRAINED LIQUID
>   8 OZ. VERY FRESH TOFU
>   ¼ CUP INSTANT NONFAT MILK POWDER
>   1 TSP. SALT
>   ¼–½ TSP. PEPPER
>   ¼ TSP. THYME
>   2 EGGS

Turn into a large bowl and stir in
    THE CLAMS
    THE COOKED VEGETABLES
    1 TBS. FINELY CHOPPED PARSLEY

Spread evenly in the prepared crust or a buttered 9″ casserole.
Bake at 350° for 30–35 minutes.
Serves 6.

STUFFED CALAMARY

THE SAUCE

Sauté in a large skillet with a cover

    1 LARGE ONION, CHOPPED FINE
    ¼ TSP. OREGANO

In

    2 TBS. OLIVE OIL

Add

    1 CAN (15 OZ.) TOMATO SAUCE
    ½ CUP DRY SHERRY
    1 TSP. FINELY CHOPPED PARSLEY
    ½ TSP. GARLIC POWDER
    ⅛ TSP. PEPPER

Bring to a boil, reduce heat and simmer, covered, for 10 minutes.

THE FILLING

Mix well in a medium-sized bowl

    1 LB. TOFU, MASHED WELL WITH A FORK OR A
      POTATO MASHER
    ¼ CUP GRATED PARMESAN CHEESE
    3 TBS. FINELY CHOPPED PARSLEY
    1 TSP. GARLIC POWDER
    ½ TSP. *EACH* BASIL AND SALT
    ¼ TSP. PEPPER

THE CALAMARY

16 SMALL SQUID, THOROUGHLY CLEANED

Stuff each long hood section ¾ full with filling.
Close hoods with toothpicks.

Brown the stuffed squid in
OLIVE OIL
Remove to sauce.

Add
TENTACLE SECTIONS, FINELY CHOPPED
(OPTIONAL)

Bring to a boil, reduce heat and simmer, covered, for 1 hour or
until tender.
Turn the squid several times during cooking.
Serves 6–8.

TOFU-MEAT ENTREES

TOFU MEAT BALLS
IN SOUR CREAM

Mix well in a large bowl
    ¾ LB. GROUND RANGE-FED BEEF
    ¾ LB. TOFU, MASHED WELL WITH A FORK OR A
      POTATO MASHER
    1 EGG, LIGHTLY BEATEN
    1½ TSP. BEEF FLAVORED BOUILLON
    ½ TSP. SALT
    ½ TSP. GARLIC POWDER
    ¼ TSP. SAGE
    ¼ TSP. PEPPER

Form into balls ½"–¾" in diameter.

Brown slowly in
    1–2 TBS. BUTTER
Place the well-browned balls in a warm 8" serving dish.

Pour GRAVY over the balls. (Recipe follows.)
Serve immediately.
Makes 4 servings.

GRAVY

Drain excess fat from the browning skillet.

Add

      1 CUP SOUR CREAM
      1 TSP. DILL WEED
      ½ TSP. HONEY
      ¼ TSP. GARLIC POWDER

Stir over low heat until hot and bubbly.

PANDANGO

Brown in a large skillet
> 1 LB. GROUND RANGE-FED BEEF

Remove beef from pan. Set aside.

Drain the pan leaving
> 1–2 TBS. FAT

Add and sauté for 2 minutes
> 1 LARGE ONION, CHOPPED
> 1 CUP CHOPPED GREEN PEPPER

Add and sauté until limp
> 3 CUPS SHREDDED CABBAGE
> 4–6 CLOVES GARLIC, MINCED OR PRESSED

Stir in
> 1 CAN (15 OZ.) TOMATO SAUCE
> 1 CUP WATER
> 1 TSP. SALT
> ½ TSP. PAPRIKA
> ¼ TSP. PEPPER
> THE MEAT
> 1 LB. TOFU, MASHED WELL WITH A FORK OR A
> POTATO MASHER
> ⅓ CUP RAISINS
> ⅔ CUP CONVERTED RICE*

Bring to a boil, reduce heat and simmer, covered, for 25 minutes.
Serves 4–6.

*Brown rice may be substituted by extending the cooking time to 1 hour.

TOFU BEEF POT

Brown lightly in a large pot with a cover
    ¾ LB. RANGE-FED BEEF, CUT IN ¼"–½"
      CUBES

Add and sauté until limp
    1 LARGE ONION, THINLY SLICED
    4–6 CLOVES GARLIC, MINCED OR PRESSED

Stir in
    5 CUPS WATER
    1 TBS. + 2 TSP. BEEF FLAVORED BOUILLON
    1 TSP. *EACH* A1 STEAK SAUCE AND
      WORCHESTERSHIRE SAUCE
    ½ TSP. *EACH* OREGANO AND THYME
    ½ BAY LEAF
    ½ TSP. SALT
    ¼–½ TSP. PEPPER
    ⅛ TSP. CLOVES
    ¼ CUP WHITE FLOUR DISSOLVED IN ½ CUP CHABLIS
      (OR APPLE JUICE)
    1 LB. FROZEN TOFU, THAWED, RINSED, SQUEEZED
      DRY AND CRUMBLED
    2½ CUPS DICED POTATOES
    1½ CUPS *EACH* CHOPPED CARROT AND CELERY

Bring to a boil, reduce heat, and simmer, covered, for 1¼ hours.
Stir occasionally.
Serves 5–6.

SAUSAGE AND TOFU
IN CASSEROLE

Pan broil
> 1½ LBS. HIGHLY SEASONED NATURAL SAUSAGE LINKS

Drain well and set aside.

Mix in a large bowl
> 2 LBS. FROZEN TOFU, THAWED, RINSED, SQUEEZED DRY AND CRUMBLED
> 10 OZ. FROZEN PEAS, SEPARATED
> 2 CUPS GRATED CHEDDAR CHEESE
> 1½ CUPS MILK
> 1 TSP. *EACH* BASIL AND OREGANO
> ¾ TSP. SALT
> ½ TSP. PEPPER
> THE SAUSAGE LINKS, CUT INTO ½" CHUNKS

Turn into a buttered 2½ quart casserole that has a cover.

Top with
> 1 CUP GRATED CHEDDAR CHEESE

Bake, covered, at 350° for 20 minutes.
Remove cover and bake for an additional 10–15 minutes—until bubbly.
Serves 6–8.

MEATY TOFU NOODLE CASSEROLE

Prepare following label instructions
> 8 OZ. WIDE EGG NOODLES

Drain well.

Sauté in a medium-sized skillet with a cover
> 1 LB. GROUND RANGE-FED BEEF
> 1 MEDIUM ONION, FINELY CHOPPED

Drain off excess fat and stir in
> 1 CAN (16 OZ.) TOMATOES, CHOPPED
> ¾ TSP. SALT
> ½ TSP. GARLIC POWDER
> ½ TSP. ITALIAN SEASONING (OR ¼ TSP. *EACH* OREGANO AND BASIL)
> ¼ TSP. PEPPER

Bring to a boil, reduce heat, and simmer, covered, for 5 minutes.

Mix well in a large bowl
> 1 LB. TOFU, MASHED WELL WITH A FORK OR A POTATO MASHER
> THE NOODLES
> ½ TSP. SALT

Spread *half* the noodle mixture in a buttered 10″ square baking dish.
Top with *half* the meat sauce.
Repeat noodle and sauce layers.
Top with
> 1 CUP GRATED SHARP CHEDDAR CHEESE

Bake at 350° for 25–30 minutes.
Serves 6–8.

LA PAZ QUICHE

THE CRUST

Mix well in a medium-sized bowl
>   1 PACKAGE (6½–7 OZ.) MEXICAN STYLE TORTILLA
>   CHIPS, CRUSHED
>   ½ CUP MELTED BUTTER

Press into a buttered 10″ spring form pan.

THE FILLING

Sauté in a large skillet over medium heat
>   ½ LB. GROUND RANGE-FED BEEF
>   1 LARGE ONION, FINELY CHOPPED
>   1 LARGE GREEN PEPPER, FINELY CHOPPED
>   2 CLOVES GARLIC, MINCED OR PRESSED

Remove from heat.

Stir in

     1 LB. TOFU, MASHED WELL WITH A FORK OR A
       POTATO MASHER
     2 CUPS GRATED SHARP CHEDDAR CHEESE
     1 CAN (7 OZ.) GREEN CHILI SALSA
     1 TBS. CHILI POWDER
     2 TSP. BEEF FLAVORED BOUILLON
     1 TSP. *EACH* CUMIN AND OREGANO
     ¾ TSP. SALT
     6 EGGS, LIGHTLY BEATEN

Turn into the prepared crust.
Bake at 375° for 25 minutes.
Serves 8–10.

BARBECUED TOFU MEAT BALLS

Mix well in a large bowl
    1½ LBS. GROUND RANGE-FED BEEF
    1½ LBS. TOFU, MASHED WELL WITH A FORK OR A
      POTATO MASHER
    1 PACKET (4 SERVING SIZE) ONION SOUP MIX
    3 TSP. DRIED PARSLEY
    ½ CUP DRIED BREAD CRUMBS
    3 EGGS, LIGHTLY BEATEN

Form into 1″ balls.
Place in a buttered 9″x12″ baking dish.

Mix in a blender until smooth
    1 CAN (8 OZ.) TOMATO SAUCE
    ½ CUP WATER
    ¼ CUP DARK BROWN SUGAR (OR 2 TBS. *EACH*
      HONEY AND LIGHT MOLASSES)
    1 TBS. + 1 TSP. PREPARED MUSTARD
    1 TSP. *EACH* CORIANDER AND GARLIC POWDER
    ¾ TSP. CUMIN
    ½ TSP. CLOVES
    ½ TSP. *EACH* ONION SALT AND SALT
    ¼ TSP. LIQUID SMOKE (OPTIONAL)

Pour evenly over the meat balls.
Bake at 350° for 1 hour.
Serves 8.

TOFU-MEAT LOAF

Mix well in a large bowl

      1½ LBS. GROUND RANGE-FED BEEF
      1 LB. TOFU, MASHED WELL WITH A FORK OR A
         POTATO MASHER
      2 EGGS, LIGHTLY BEATEN
      ¼ CUP FINE DRIED BREAD CRUMBS
      ¼ CUP CATSUP
      2 TBS. DEHYDRATED ONION FLAKES
      2 TSP. WORCHESTERSHIRE SAUCE
      1½ TSP. SALT
      ½ TSP. GARLIC POWDER
      ¼–½ TSP. PEPPER
      ¼ TSP. BITTERS (OPTIONAL)

Turn into a buttered 9"x5" loaf pan.
Bake at 350° for 1½ hours.
Serves 6–8.

TOFU BREAD AND DESSERTS

DIETER'S LIGHT AND EASY GRIDDLE CAKES

Mix in a blender until smooth
- 8 EGGS
- 1 LB. VERY FRESH TOFU
- 2 TBS. HONEY
- 1 TSP. VANILLA
- ¼ TSP. SALT
- ½ CUP FLOUR

Bake on a lightly buttered, medium-hot griddle until done.
Makes about 36 griddle cakes.

TOFU BISCUITS

Mix well in a large bowl
>   1¾ CUP WHOLEWHEAT FLOUR (OR 1 CUP
>   WHOLEWHEAT AND ¾ CUP UNBLEACHED FLOUR)
>   2 TBS. DARK BROWN SUGAR
>   2 TSP. BAKING POWDER
>   ½ TSP. BAKING SODA
>   ½ TSP. SALT

Cut in with a pastry blender or 2 knives
>   2 TBS. SOFT BUTTER

Stir or work in with hands
>   1 CUP (8 OZ.) TOFU, MASHED WELL WITH A FORK
>   OR A POTATO MASHER
>   1 EGG, LIGHTLY BEATEN

Pat or roll out dough to ½″ thickness on a floured surface.
Cut with a biscuit cutter.
Bake on a buttered baking sheet at 450° for 15–18 minutes.
Makes about 10 large biscuits.

These biscuits freeze very well. To reheat wrap in aluminum foil.

SAN DIEGO
APPLE-SPICE DELIGHT

Soak

     1 SALTED MATZO CRACKER (OR 2 SLICES DRIED
     BREAD), BROKEN UP

In

     ½ CUP MILK

Mix well in a medium-sized bowl
     4 EGGS, LIGHTLY BEATEN
     8 OZ. VERY FRESH TOFU, MASHED WELL WITH A
     FORK OR A POTATO MASHER
     1 LARGE APPLE, GRATED
     2 TBS. HONEY
     ½ TSP. *EACH* CINNAMON AND VANILLA
     ¼ TSP. SALT

Gently stir in the soaked matzo or bread.
Turn into a buttered 8″ round baking pan.
Bake at 375° for 20–25 minutes or until set.

Great with butter and maple syrup.
Serves 3.

BANANA COCONUT CAKE

Mix well in a large bowl
> 1½ CUPS WHOLEWHEAT FLOUR
> 1 CUP UNBLEACHED FLOUR
> 2 TSP. BAKING SODA
> 1 CUP UNSWEETENED COCONUT
> 1 CUP CHOPPED WALNUTS (OPTIONAL)

Mix in a blender until smooth. Use a spatula to keep the mixture in the blades if necessary.
> 2 EGGS
> ⅔ CUP *EACH* BUTTER AND HONEY
> ½ CUP (4 OZ.) CREAM CHEESE
> ½ CUP INSTANT NONFAT MILK POWDER
> 1 TSP. VANILLA
> 8 OZ. VERY FRESH TOFU

Pour the blended ingredients into the flour mixture.

Add
> 3 VERY RIPE BANANAS, MASHED WELL WITH A FORK

Mix well.

Turn into a 10″ buttered and floured spring form pan.
Bake at 350° for 45 minutes.

GINGERED NECTAR PUDDING

Mix well in a large bowl
>½ CUP HONEY
>1 TSP. LEMON JUICE
>2 TBS. FLOUR
>¾ TSP. CINNAMON
>½ TSP. GINGER
>¼ TSP. SALT
>4 CUPS THINLY SLICED PEARS

Turn into a buttered 8″ square baking dish.

Dot with
>1 TBS. BUTTER (OPTIONAL)

Mix in a blender until smooth
>3 EGGS
>6 TBS. FROZEN ORANGE JUICE CONCENTRATE
>12 OZ. VERY FRESH TOFU
>½ CUP HONEY
>½ TSP. GRATED LEMON RIND
>1 TSP. VANILLA
>½ TSP. CINNAMON
>¼ TSP. GINGER

Gently pour the blended ingredients over the pears.
Do not stir.

Bake at 350° for 40 minutes.
Serve warm or chilled.

WALNUT PIE

THE CRUST (OPTIONAL)

Prepare your favorite single 9″ crust.
Bake at 400° for 8 minutes.

THE FILLING

Mix in a blender until smooth
    2 EGGS
    12 OZ. VERY FRESH TOFU
    ¼ CUP BUTTER, SOFTENED
    ¼ CUP LIGHT MOLASSES
    1 TSP. VANILLA
    1 TBS. RUM (OR ⅛ TSP. RUM EXTRACT)
    ¼ TSP. SALT
    1 CUP DARK BROWN SUGAR, PACKED

Stir in well with a long handled spoon
    1½ CUPS COARSELY CHOPPED WALNUTS
Turn into the pie shell or a buttered 9″ baking dish.

Bake at 350° for 45 minutes.
Chill thoroughly.

PEANUT BUTTER PIE

THE CRUST (OPTIONAL)

Prepare your favorite single 9" crust.
Bake as needed and cool completely.

THE FILLING

Soften
>   2 TBS. UNFLAVORED GELATIN

In
>   ¼ CUP WATER

Heat to dissolve completely.

Mix in a blender until smooth
>   3 EGG YOLKS
>   1 LB. VERY FRESH TOFU
>   ¾ CUP HONEY
>   ¼ CUP LIGHT MOLASSES
>   ½ CUP PEANUT BUTTER
>   1 TSP. VANILLA
>   THE GELATIN MIXTURE
>   A DASH OF SALT (ADD ½ TSP. SALT IF PEANUT
>   BUTTER USED IS UNSALTED)

In a medium-sized bowl beat stiff
>   3 EGG WHITES

Gently fold the egg whites into the tofu ingredients.
Turn into the prepared crust.
Chill thoroughly before serving.

EGG NOG TORTE

THE CRUST (OPTIONAL)

Prepare your favorite crumb crust in an 8″ spring form pan.

THE FILLING

Mix in a blender until smooth
- 1½ CUPS EGG NOG
- 8 OZ. VERY FRESH TOFU
- 2 EGGS
- ⅓ CUP HONEY
- 2 TBS. BRANDY

Turn into the prepared crust or a buttered 8″ baking dish.

Bake at 325° for 1 hour.
Chill thoroughly.

PERFECTION PLUM PRIZE

THE CRUST

Mix well in a medium-sized bowl
      1½ CUPS UNBLEACHED FLOUR
      ¼ CUP BROWN SUGAR
      ¼ TSP. SALT

Cut in with a pastry blender or 2 knives
      ½ CUP BUTTER, SOFTENED

Work with hands to form a ball.
Press the dough into the bottom of a buttered 9"x9"x2" baking pan.

FRUIT FILLING

Mix well in a medium-sized bowl
      4 CUPS THINLY SLICED ITALIAN PRUNE PLUMS*
      2 TBS. FLOUR
      ½ CUP HONEY
      1½ TSP. CINNAMON

Spread over the prepared crust.

*When plums are out of season try golden delicious apples instead.

THE CUSTARD

Mix in a blender until smooth
>   2 EGGS
>   ½ CUP HONEY
>   12 OZ. VERY FRESH TOFU
>   ½ CUP (4 OZ.) CREAM CHEESE
>   1½ TSP. VANILLA
>   ½ TSP. CINNAMON
>   ½ TSP. GRATED LEMON RIND

Gently pour the blended ingredients over the fruit.
Do not stir.

Bake at 350° for 1 hour.
Chill thoroughly before serving.

CAFE AU LAIT CHEESECAKE

THE CRUST (OPTIONAL)

Prepare your favorite cheesecake crumb crust in an 8″ spring form
pan or a 10″ pie pan.
Bake if necessary.
Chill until needed.

THE FILLING

Soften
        2 TBS. UNFLAVORED GELATIN

In
        ½ CUP WATER
Heat to dissolve completely.

Stir in
        3 TBS. INSTANT COFFEE FLAVORED POWDER

Mix in a blender until smooth
        2 EGG YOLKS
        1 LB. VERY FRESH TOFU
        1 CUP HONEY
        1 CUP (8 OZ.) CREAM CHEESE, SOFTENED
        1 TSP. VANILLA
        ¼ TSP. SALT
        THE GELATIN MIXTURE

In a medium-sized bowl beat stiff
    2 EGG WHITES

In another bowl whip
    1 CUP WHIPPING CREAM

Pour the tofu ingredients into a large bowl.
Gently fold both the egg whites and the whipped cream into the tofu ingredients.

Turn into the prepared crust or a pudding mold.
Chill overnight.

MOCHA CHEESECAKE

Prepare CAFE AU LAIT CHEESECAKE filling.

Add with other blender ingredients
    2 TBS. UNSWEETENED COCOA

Enjoy!

TOFABALA

CREAM CHEESE CRUST

Using an electric mixer, cream together in a large bowl
    1 CUP (8 OZ.) CREAM CHEESE
    ½ CUP BUTTER
    ¼ CUP BROWN SUGAR, LIGHTLY PACKED
    1 TSP. VANILLA
    ½ TSP. SALT

Mix in
    2 CUPS FLOUR
Press the dough into a buttered 9"x12" baking dish bringing it ½"
up the sides.
Flute the edges.

THE FILLING

Mix well in a large bowl
    1 LB. FROZEN TOFU, THAWED, RINSED, SQUEEZED
      DRY AND CRUMBLED
    1 CUP BROWN SUGAR, FIRMLY PACKED
    ½ CUP *EACH* CHOPPED ALMONDS AND WALNUTS
    ⅓ CUP *EACH* RAISINS AND CHOPPED DATES
    1 TSP. CINNAMON
    ¼ TSP. SALT
Turn into the prepared crust.

Dot with
    2 TBS. BUTTER

Bake at 350° for 1 hour.

APPENDIX*

*Excerpted from TOFU GOES WEST, ©1978

TOFU:
A NUTRITIONAL PROFILE

8 OUNCES OF TOFU PROVIDE THE FOLLOWING: *

calories. 164.0
protein . . . . 17.6 g
fat. . . . . 9.6 g
carbohydrate . . . . 5.4 g
calcium . . . . 292.0 mg
phosphorus. . . . . 286.0 mg
iron . . . . 4.4 mg
sodium . . . . 96.0 mg
potassium . . . . 96.0 mg
thiamine . . . . 0.12 mg
riboflavin . . . . 0.08 mg

*Source: COMPOSITION OF FOODS, Agriculture Handbook No. 8, Agricultural Research Service, U.S. Dept. of Agriculture, 1963.

8 ounces of tofu provide the same amount of usable protein as *

    3¼ oz. steak . . . . at the cost of . . . . 230 calories
    5½ oz. hamburger . . . . . at the cost of . . . . 440 calories
    1⅔ cup milk . . . . at the cost of . . . . 220 calories
    2 eggs . . . . at the cost of . . . . 160 calories
    2 oz. cheese . . . . at the cost of . . . . 200 calories

8 ounces of tofu provide about the same amount of calcium as **

    8 oz. of milk – Great for people who don't like or can't drink milk!

8 ounces of tofu provide about the same amount of iron as **

    4½ eggs . . . . at the cost of . . . . 360 calories
    2 oz. beef liver . . . . at the cost of . . . . . 80 calories

*Shurtleff, William, and Aoyagi, Akiko, THE BOOK OF TOFU, Autumn Press, U.S.A., 1975, page 25.

**Source: COMPOSITION OF FOODS, Agriculture Handbook No. 8, Agricultural Research Service, U.S. Dept. of Agriculture, 1963.

RECIPE INDEX

Other FRESH PRESS Books

THE BUSY PEOPLE'S NATURALLY NUTRITIOUS DECIDEDLY
DELICIOUS FAST FOODBOOK

TOFU GOES WEST

DINNER CAN BE A PICNIC ALL YEAR ROUND (Fall 1981)